Christmas c[rafts] decorations: trees, wreaths, candle holders and christmas balls.

An easy guide step by step with photos

The
Susanna Catena
Collection

2019 © Susanna Catena

All rights reserved

Index:

Introduction 4

Crochet Christmas balls 8

Introduction 9

Christmas ball fur effect in lurex 11

Red and gold Christmas ball 24

Romantic Christmas ball 35

Crochet christmas trees 43

Introduction 44

Shabby chic crochet christmas wreath 63

Introduction 64

Crochet christmas Candle holder 85

Introduction 86

Introduction

Here he comes back: Christmas is coming!

The days get shorter and the evenings get longer. This period is also characterized by the joyful expectation of light. We hug each other, we warm ourselves with candle lights and the fireplace. We sweeten the wait with hot drinks and spices that warm up like cinnamon, cloves and cardamom. We prepare Christmas cakes and biscuits and ... rediscover the crochet hook!

In this collection I have included a wide range of proposals for crochet lovers.

For most people the Christmas tree is the most beautiful Christmas symbol and obviously the most passionate of the crochet works will want to show off their creativity also in the realization of the decorations for their Christmas tree.

For this reason, Christmas balls could not be missing in this collection; the Christmas decorations par excellence proposed in 3 variants!

There are also beautiful soft saplings to hang even in the Christmas tree or where you prefer to beautify the house.

For your Christmas table, I propose star-shaped candle holders that can be used in the center of the table to enrich it or as a placeholder for every person present at our table.

Finally, the unmistakable touch of elegance of the shabby could not be missing, brought back into a Christmas context to make everything shine with refinement, with a wreath to hang outside the front door to welcome all our guests!

Crochet is fun!

Just start a job to see it grow quickly: it will be ready in a short time!

I have collected the most beautiful models: let yourself be inspired.

In any case, the fun is guaranteed !!

For these splendid decorative models only a little crochet skill is required, but also a little familiarity with bricolage. So, let's go for manual work.

I can only wish you good fun and happy holidays !!!!

Crochet Christmas balls

Introduction

This year, for the Christmas holidays, decorate your home with handmade festive crocheted decorations!

Oh yes, Christmas time is almost here, and with it comes the joy for this season of the year! If you like the small decorations that give the house that party atmosphere, this is the best way to express your love for the Christmas holidays. And what better way than to create these decorations alone? Crochet is a fun and fantastic way to express your creativity.

In this book you will find 3 projects for fantastic and particular Christmas balls, to hang on the tree or where you prefer. Complete instructions are provided and explained step by step on how to work with crochet, and each step is photographed, so that the reader can clearly see how to do it. These Christmas balls are easy and achievable in a short time, also suitable for those inexperienced or for those who have just started to crochet.

Have fun with the process, show off your love for the season, and get into the groove of the Christmas spirit; it only happens once a year, and perhaps for this reason, it is also the best time of the year!

So get your crochet hook and your favorite yarn and get to work! With my patterns you will discover that all this is really easy and fun !!

Christmas ball fur effect in lurex

Materials:

- 50 gr. (1.76 oz_) of white acrylic wool
- 30 gr. (1.06 oz) of gold or silver lurex fur effect yarn
- Decorative ribbon in gold organza or other color to taste
- Transparent Christmas ball of cm. 8 or 9 (3.15/3.54 in)
- Crochet n.3
- Wool needle
- Scissors
- Hot spray gun and hot glue

Execution:

- Work with both yarns!

1st RND:

- Start chain 4 and close them in a circle;

- In the circle, work chain 3 (which replace the first double crochet),

then work double crochet 9.

(See photo):

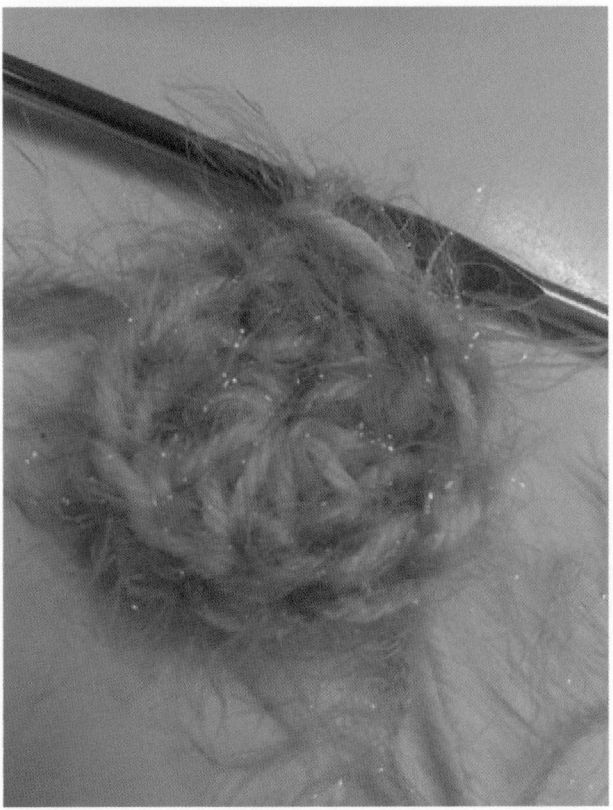

At this point, close the loop by aiming the crochet hook in the third starting chain.

2nd RND:

work chain 3 (which replace the first double crochet), then work 1 increase in each double crochet below. 2 double crochet in each double crochet. (See photo):

Close the lap always making a slip stitch on the third chain of the lap below.

3rd RND:

work 1 double crochet and in the next 2 double crochet at the same point, then alternate these 2 steps all the way around.

(See photo):

4th RND:

We alternate 2 double crochet and 1 increase (2 double crochet in the same double crochet) for the whole lap we close with 1 slip stitch in the chain 3 at the beginning of the lap below.

(See photo):

5 th e 6 th RND:

without increases, 1 double crochet in each double crochet below

(See photo):

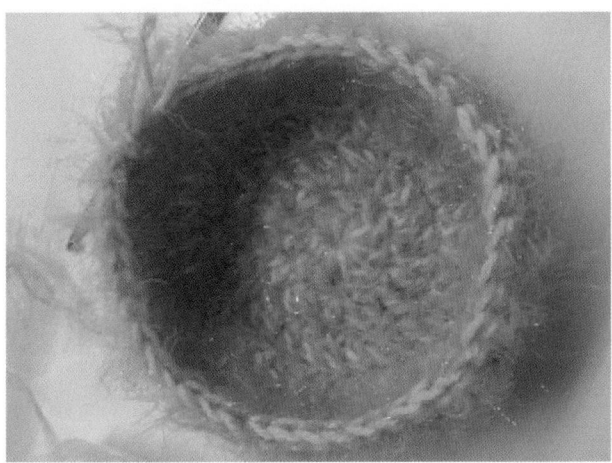

From this moment on we will work with the sphere inside the work!

7 th RND:

we start the round by always making 3 initial chains (which replace the first double crochet); and let's start the decreases like this:

2 double crochet in the following 2 double crochet, 1 decrease (2 double crochet closed together) for the whole ride.

(See photo):

8 th RND:

now we alternate 1 double crochet and 1 decrease (2 double crochet closed together) for the whole lap.

(See photo):

9 th RND:

only decreases (2 double crochet closed together) for the whole ride.

(See photo):

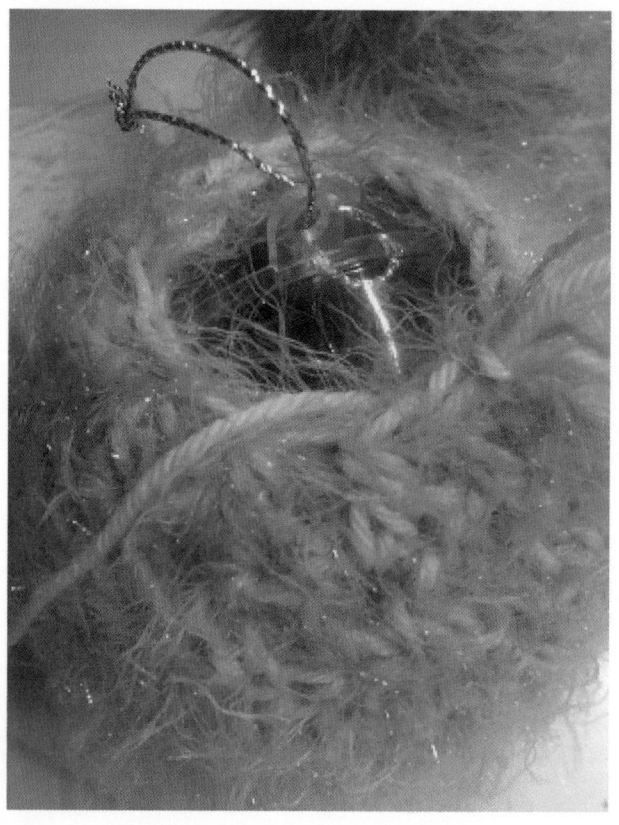

10 th RND:

only decreases (2 double crochet closed together) for the whole ride.

(See photo):

Our ball is finished, it only remains to disperse the extra threads with a wool needle.

(See photo):

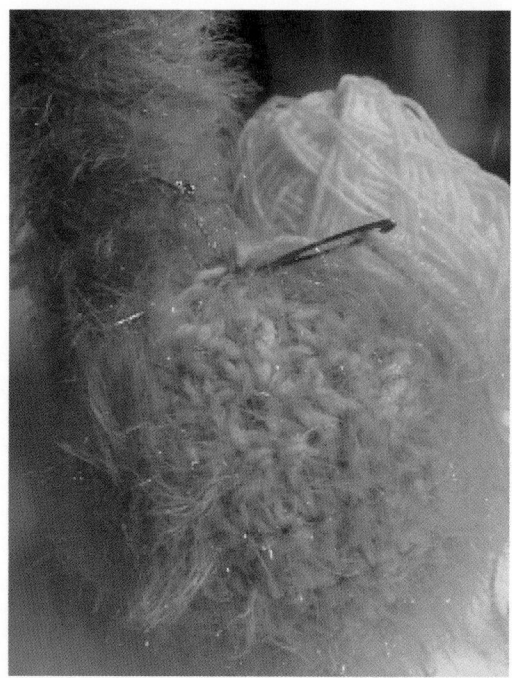

At last, apply the organza ribbon, making a bow and attach it with a hot glue tip to the upper center of the ball.

(See photo):

Adjust the fur processing with your hands.

The Christmas ball is ready to hang from your tree or wherever you like!!

Red and gold Christmas ball

Materials:

- 20 grams (0.71 oz) of red cotton n. 8

- crochet No. 1.50

- a transparent Christmas ball with a diameter of 8 cm (3.15 in)

- A few grams of gold lurex thread

- red bow or other color to taste in organza

- scissors.

Execution:

1st RND:

Make chains 20 and close them in a circle,

in the circle work 1 single crochet and chains 3, 1 single crochet and chains 3, until the end of the turn;

close the lap with 1 slip stitch in the last single crochet.

It is necessary to obtain 12 small arches of 3 chains.

(See photo):

2nd RND:

Inside the arch of 3 chains, work 1 double crochet - chains 2, 1 double crochet - chain 1 and inside the following arch work again 1 double crochet – chains 2 and 1 double crochet – chain 1, until the end of the turn.

(See photo):

3 rd RND:

With a slip stitch reach the arch below, then make 2 double crochet – chains 2, 2 double crochet – chain 1, and in the following arch make still 2 double crochet - chains 2, and 2 double crochet – chain 1, until the end of the turn.

(See photo):

4th RND:

Inside the first arch of the lap below make 1 single crochet and flying chains 12, 1 single crochet in the following arch then with some slip stitch go up to the following arch and inside make 1 single crochet and flying chains 12 and 1 single crochet in the following arch until the end of the turn.

(See photo):

5th RND:

Inside the arch of 12 chains make 12 double crochet - flying chains 25, and then aim the crochet hook in the twelfth double crochet, and make 1 slip stitch, then make another 12 double crochet always in the same arch;

in the following space make 1 single crochet and next arch repeat again the same sequence: 12 double crochet - flying chains 25; aim the crochet hook in the twelfth double crochet, and make 1 slip stitch, then make another 12 double crochet , continue like this until the end of the tour.

(See photo):

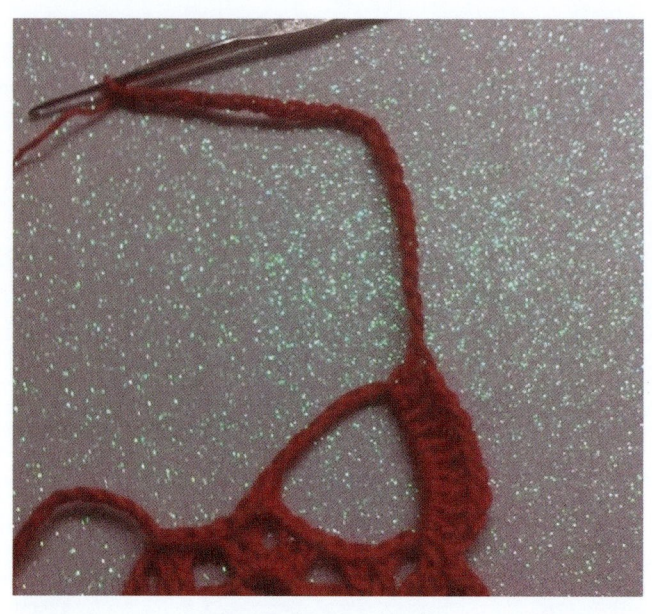

6th AND LAST RND:

Finish with a round of single crochet for all the way around with the gold lurex yarn.

(See photo):

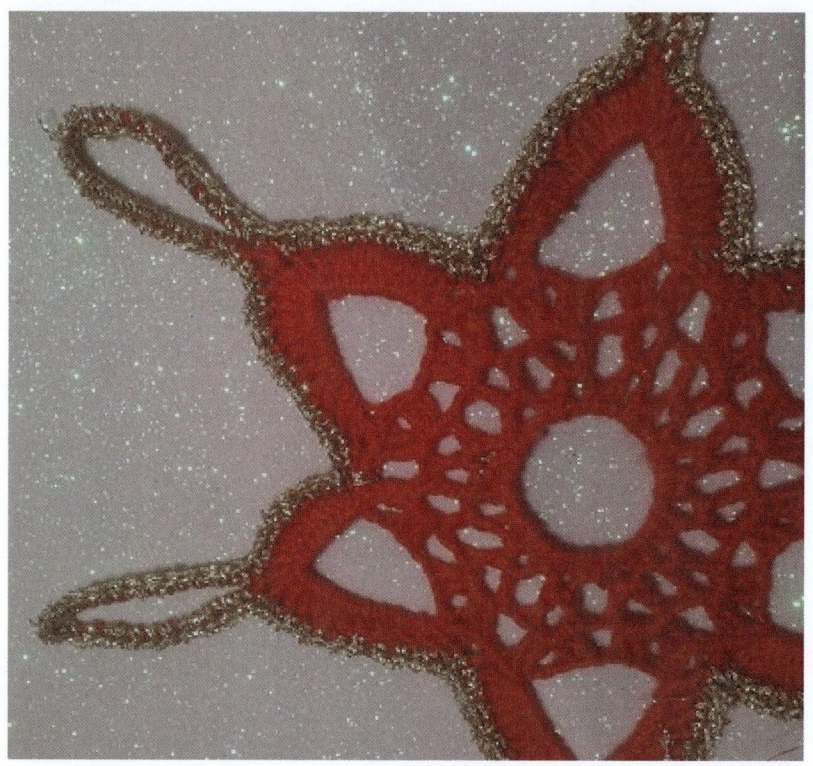

ASSEMBLY:

Place the ball on the work table and pass the ribbon through the slots formed by the flying chains.

(See photo):

Then carefully pull the ribbon over the ends of the ball and make the ribbon.

(See photo):

This Christmas ball is also ready to hang wherever you like!!!

Romantic Christmas ball

Materials:

- Acrylic wool about 50 grams (1.76 oz)
- a polystyrene sphere with a diameter of 7 or 8 cm (2.76 in or 3.15 in)
- white satin ribbon to hang the ball
- 25 pins with pearls
- crochet No. 2,5
- scissors
- hot glue

Execution:

Make a magic circle and make 14 double crochet inside. (See photo):

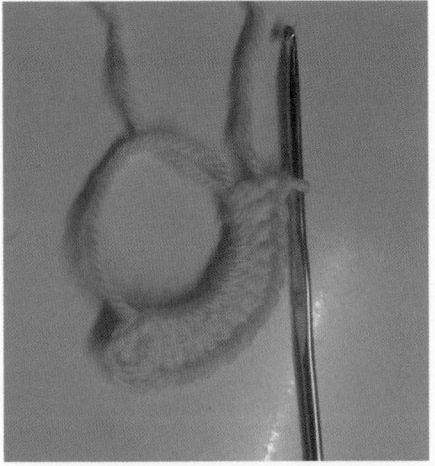

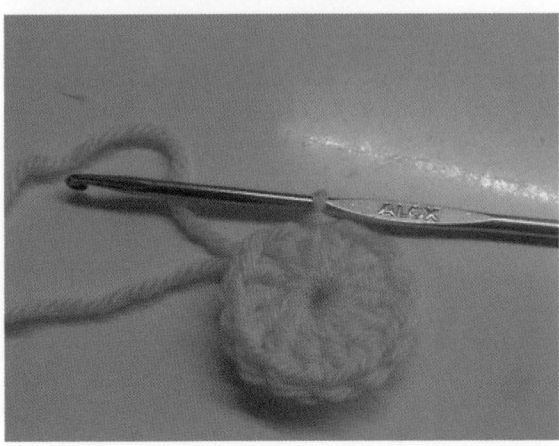

Close with 1 slip stitch –chains 3, and in the following point 1 slip stitch- chains 3, and in the following point 1 slip stitch.

Continue like this until the end of the lap and finish with 1 slip stitch at the last point.

(See photo):

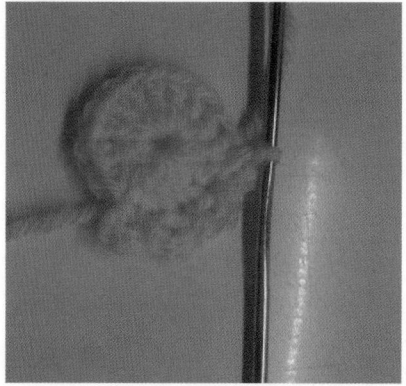

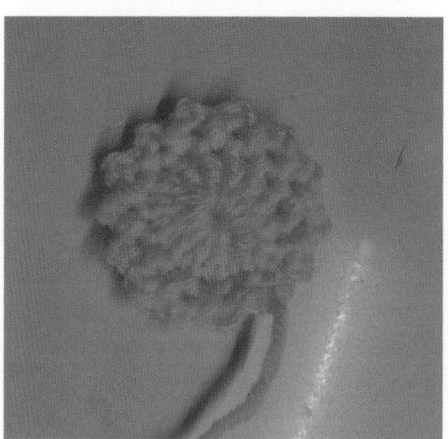

make about 25 small flowers, remember that depending on the yarn (more or less thin) the number of flowers may vary.

Assembly :

with hot glue, attach the satin ribbon to the end of the sphere.
 (See photo):

We begin to fill the sphere with the little flowers with a pin in the center of the flower.

(See photo):

Continue like this until completely covering the sphere.

(See photo):

With this method you can make colored variants with lurex yarns and colored pins

and all that imagination suggests to you !!!

Good creativity !!!!

Crochet christmas trees

Introduction

Let's get ready to open the doors to this Christmas that is coming!!!

One of the best ways is undoubtedly to help make the environment of our houses joyful and festive with the small handmade crochet creations, putting our imagination and creativity at stake.

These trees can be used in many ways.

First you can hang on the Christmas tree, waiting for it to fill with gifts, you can alternate with the classic Christmas balls or fill your tree only with these trees of various colors! But they can also be placed on the doorstep or behind the doors of our apartments and why not, even on the walls. In addition, processed with thinner yarn can become keychains to give as gifts or can be used as a placeholder on the Christmas table.

You can use traditional Christmas colors or the tones of the timeless Chic shabby style !!!

In short, the uses that can be done are many ... everything now depends on your imagination !!

Take the crochet hook and good job !!!!

Tree size : 3,93 x 4,72 in

- **Material required:**

- cotton yarn n° 5;
- crochet n° 2;
- padding wadding;
- organza or satin ribbon;
- scissors;
- wool needle;
- cord to hang the tree

Execution:

The constants of this project are as follows:

- Take a round trip and one return;

- Always turn the work around every lap;

- Always make 5 double crochet at the center of the job, all in the same base point;

- Always start the round trip and the return with 2 double crochet in the first base point.

Pattern:

-

Repeat the following scheme twice:

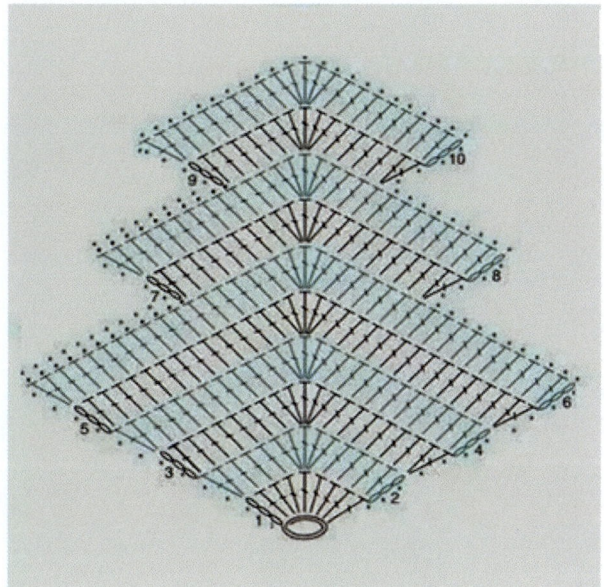

And now that we have everything … .take the crochet hook in hand and start !!!

1st round:

Start a magic ring, and inside it work 9 double crochet (the first double crochet is always replaced by 3 chains).

(See photo):

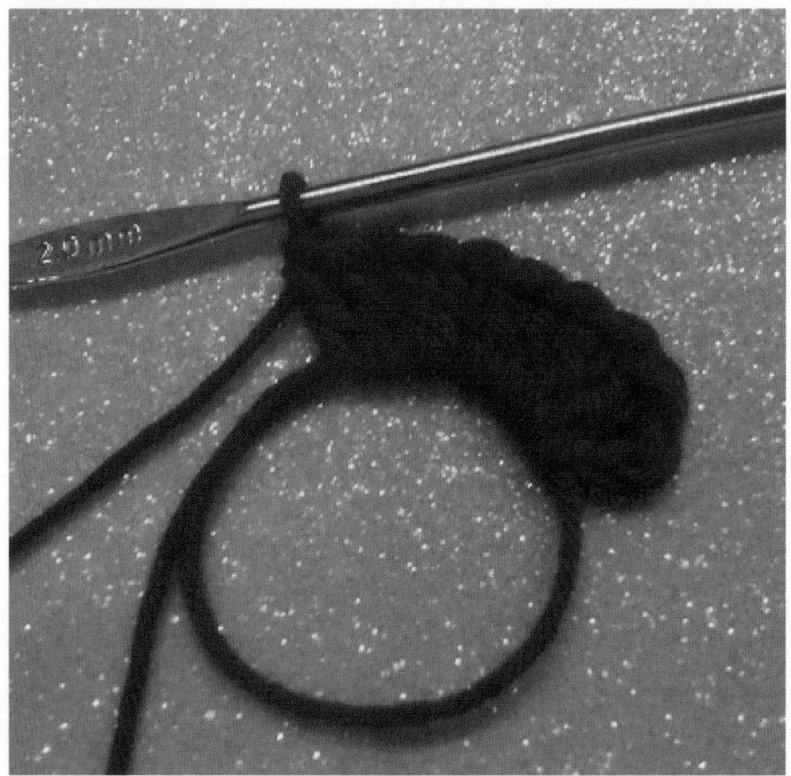

2nd round:

2 double crochet at the same point, 3 double crochet above the points below,
5 double crochet all in the same central point of the previous lap,
3 double crochet, 2 double crochet together in the same point.

(See photo):

3rd round:

2 double crochet in the same point, 6 double crochet above the points below,
5 double crochet all in the same central point of the previous lap,
6 double crochet, 2 double crochet together in the same point.

(See photo):

4th round:

2 double crochet at the same point, 9 double crochet above the points below,
5 double crochet all in the same central point of the previous lap,
9 double crochet, 2 double crochet together in the same point.

(See photo):

5th round:

2 double crochet at the same point, 12 double crochet above the points below,
5 double crochet all in the same central point of the previous lap,
12 double crochet, 2 double crochet together in the same point.

(See photo):

6th round:

2 double crochet at the same point, 15 double crochet above the points below,
5 double crochet all in the same central point of the previous lap,
15 double crochet, 2 double crochet together in the same point.

(See photo):

At this point it is necessary to break the thread and enter with the crochet hook in the tenth point of the triangle. Now you can start the seventh round.

7th round:

2 double crochet at the same point, 7 double crochet above the points below,
5 double crochet all in the same central point of the previous lap,
7 double crochet, 2 double crochet together in the same point.

(See photo):

8th round:

2 double crochet at the same point, 10 double crochet above the points below,
5 double crochet all in the same central point of the previous lap,
10 double crochet, 2 double crochet together in the same point.
 (See photo):

 Even now you have to break the thread and enter with the hook in the tenth point of the triangle below.
Now you can start the ninth round.

9th round:

2 double crochet in the same point, 4 double crochet above the points below,
5 double crochet all in the same central point of the previous lap,
4 double crochet, 2 double crochet together in the same point.

(See photo):

10th round:

2 double crochet at the same point, 7 double crochet above the points below,
5 double crochet all in the same central point of the previous lap,
7 double crochet, 2 double crochet together in the same point.

(See photo):

Now we have to make another small tree like the one we have just done, so we have to overlap them and make a single crochet lap around the perimeter, taking care to make 2 single crochet at the same point in all the corners of the tree.

(See photo):

Before closing the work insert the wadding and the tape. (See photo):

And here is finished my tree !!!
Now to embellish think about it !!!
Good creativity !!!!

Shabby chic crochet christmas wreath

Introduction

For Christmas, there's nothing better than decorating your home with this beautiful Shabby Chic style Christmas wreath!

Hang it out the door to show everyone ... your creations!

The colors of the wreath, in perfect shabby chic style, give a touch of elegance to the home. It is perfect as a front door or as an interior decoration, it is the ideal gift for Christmas holidays. This shabby chic wreath is a single piece like all my works and is embellished with various decorations. It is handmade crochet with particular finishes and attention to detail. It's very easy to do and it can be done in a short time.... you just have to take the crochet and start creating !!!!

Material:

•

-white acrylic wool

-cotton yarn: antique pink and beige

- silver lurex yarn

- crochet n° 2,5

-wool needle

-polystyrene wreath: diameter of 8,66 in

-various pins

-various decorations (strands of pearls or various pearls, fir branches, silver branches, silver and pink ribbons, silver glitter ball, plastic ice flakes)

-Hot glue

Execution:

•

Make a panel as long as the perimeter of the wreath and as wide as its circumference, single crochet in back loop. (if you have a wreath like mine of 8,66 in, otherwise lengthen and widen the panel in proportion to the circumference of your wreath in polystyrene).

Start 20 chains,

go back to single crochet until the end of the lap,

then make a chain and turn the work previous, always single crochet, however, in back loop, that is taking back loop only.

Continue with round trips to the desired length.

See photos:

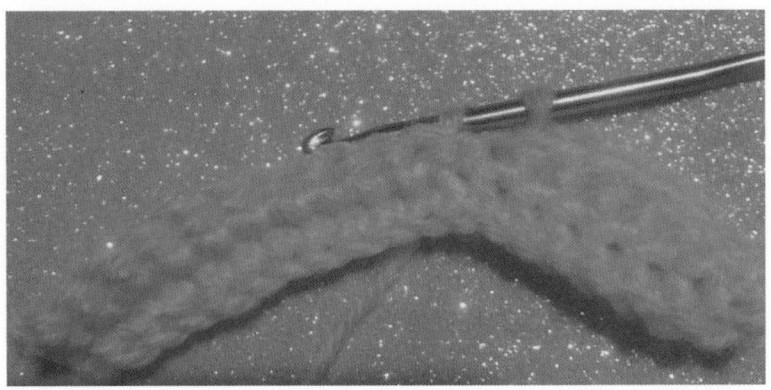

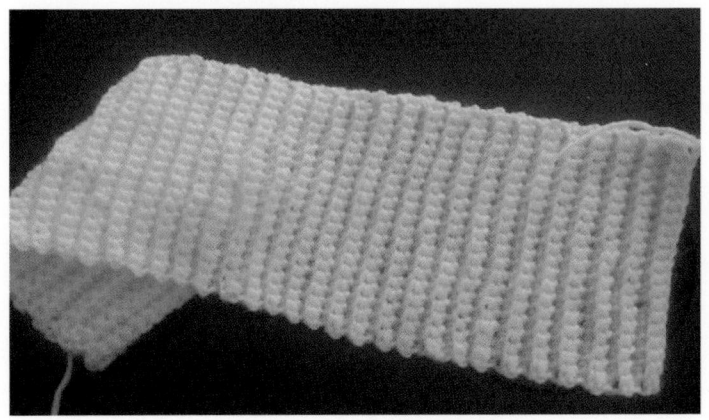

-How to sew the panel in the wreath:

Place the panel around the wreath;

join the panel with a seam with needle and white wool yarn;

See photo:

With the help of pins, attach the panel well and sew from one side and the other as in the photos:

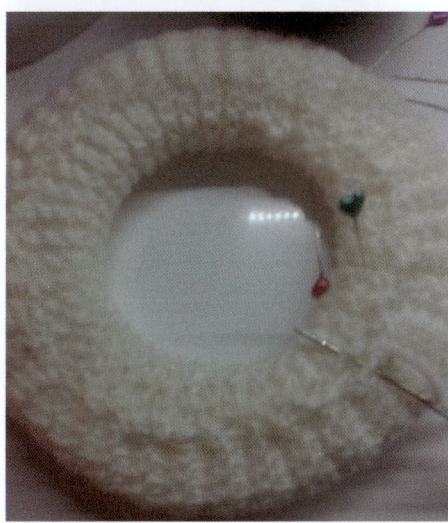

On the front of the work the wreath should be like this:

At this point the base of the Christmas wreath is finished; put it aside and proceed with the Christmas star.

-With the antique pink cotton and a thin silver lurex yarn joined together, we start 9 chains.

1st round:

1 single crochet in the second chain from the crochet,

1 single crochet in each of the next 6 chains,

3 single crochet all in the last chain,

working on the opposite side, in the slots left free of the basic chain:

1 single crochet, in each of the 6 buttonholes.

2nd round:

2 chains,

turn (working in back loop only) and skip a single crochet,

1 single crochet in each of the next 6 single crochet,

3 single crochet all in the next stitch,

1 single crochet (going down on the opposite side) in each of the 6 single crochet.

Repeat x 4 in total.

See photos:

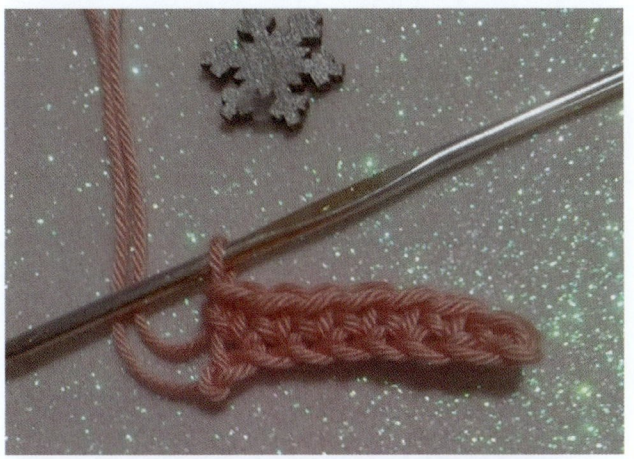

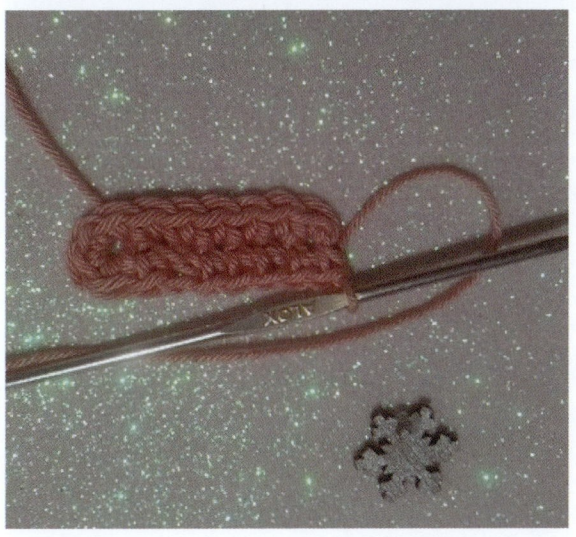

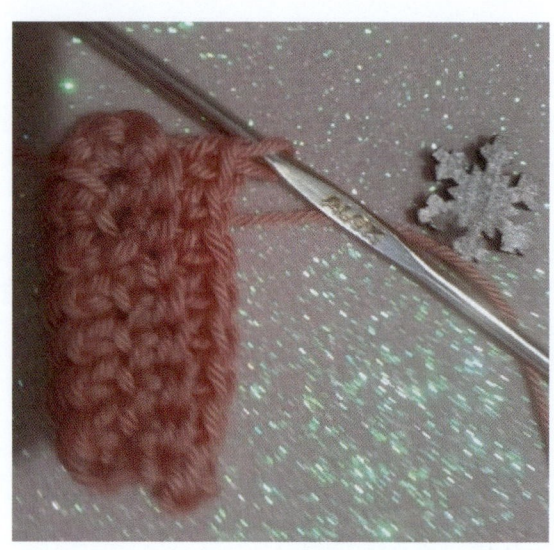

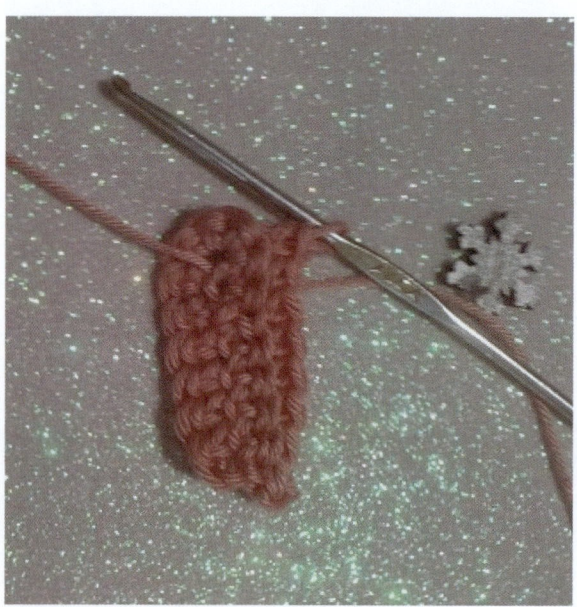

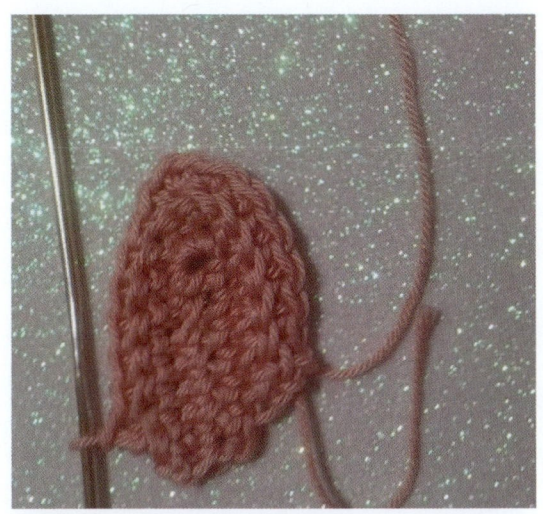

-To make two other leaves like these with the same process, but with the beige color and the lurex yarn together.

-Assemby:

Wrap the Christmas garland with a string of pearls, alternatively you can attach with the hot glue of the pearls.

See photos:

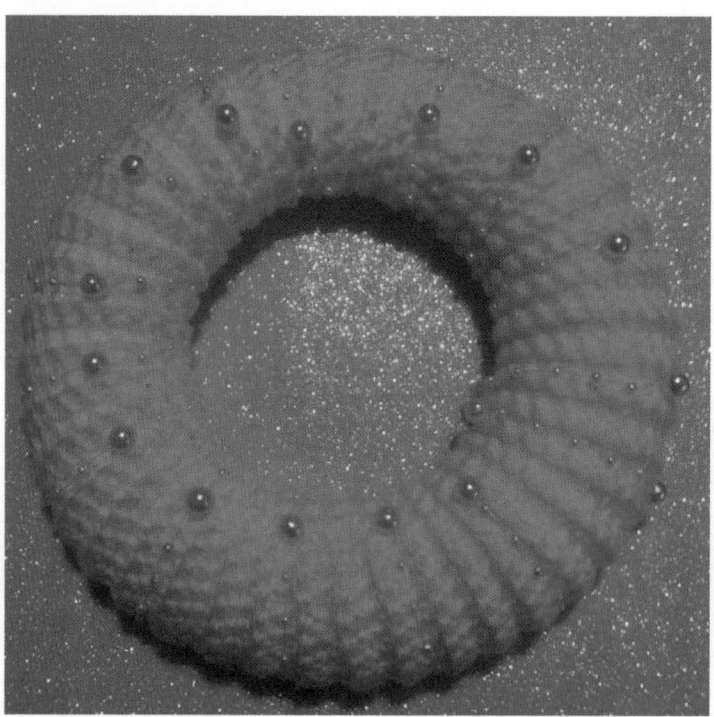

With the pink leaves form a Christmas star and attach a small silver ball to the center of the star, then attach the star in the Christmas wreath with hot glue.

On the sides of the star attach two beige leaves, then between the star and the leaves, glue two small pine branches and if you have some silver ice crystals (or what you find in the Christmas decorations you have at home that you like) .

See photos:

Attach two silver branches to the sides of the composition.

See photos:

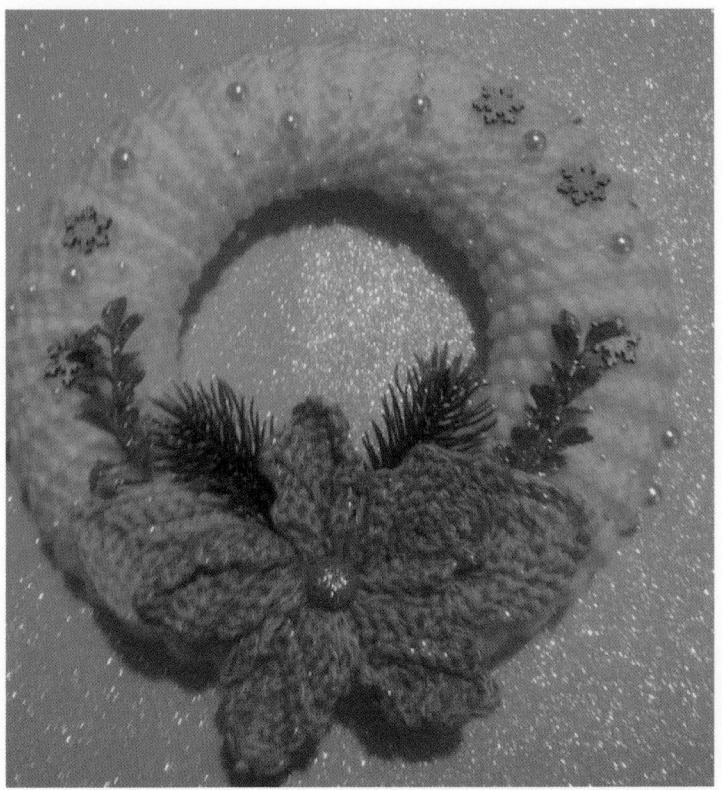

Insert a large silver ribbon in the center of the wreath.

Now we just have to attach a second smaller antique rose ribbon and the work is finished, of course the decorations are to your taste so let loose with your imagination !!

See photos:

Good creative work and happy holidays !!!

Crochet christmas Candle holder

Introduction

The time has come to start concentrating and thinking about how our table should be on Christmas Day, how to decorate and decorate it in the best possible way or how to welcome our guests on the most important and festive day of the year!

This time I propose a beautiful model of candle holder made with tips that make it look like a star.

You can create them in any color and they will be perfect for all seasons ... But then just add a touch of lurex gold, red or silver and it will be immediately party ...!!

All you have to do is get to work: it only takes a little time and little material to see your candle holders completed.

In addition, given their small size, they can also be used as placeholders on the Christmas table.

Just a little imagination and a few grams of lurex cotton will make your table nice, original and welcoming, ready to pick up guests and delicious dishes that will wait for us in these happy days of celebration, which we all expect...

- **Material required:**

- 16 grams of lurex jute or other yarn as desired
- Crochet no. 4
- 1 round candle with a diameter of 3.5 cm.

The diameter of the finished candle holder will be about 10cm.

Proceeding:

1st lap:

Start a magic circle and work inside it 3 chains (which replace the first double crochet) and 19 other double crochet, for a total of 20 double crochet.

(See photo):

Close by making 1 slip stitch on the 3 chain of the initial stitch.

(See photo):

2nd round:

Point the crochet hook at the first double crochet and run 3 chains.

(replacing the first double crochet) then another 19 double crochet but taken in the back coast.

(See photo):

After the double crochet have been made, close with 1 slip stitch in the 3 chain of the first starting stitch,

we'll have created the candle house.

(See photo):

3rd round:

Turn the work upside down, and perform in the coast remained free of the previous lap, 20 slip stitch.

(See photo):

At this point, close the lap with a slip stitch.

4th and final round:

A single crochet in the first stitch of the underlying lap.

Skip one chain, and in the next, make 3 double crochet separated by 3 chains all in the same stitch,

then skip another stitch and perform a single crochet ,

jump a stitch and make 3 double crochet separated by 3 chains; continue in this way until the end of the lap.

Close with 1 slip stitch on the single crochet of the lap below.

(See photo):

Our candle holder is finished, a very simple and fast project but of great effect.

Placeholder candle holder

Here's the placeholder variant!!!

- **Material required:**

- Lurex yarn
- Crochet no. 4
- Wool needle
- Scissors
- Round candles with a diameter of 3.5 cm.

Each candle holder weighs about 8 grams and has a diameter of 7 cm from tip to tip.

Proceeding:

The procedure is the same as for the jute candle holder; the difference lies in the dimensions, as being a placeholder, it must be smaller than the jute one in order to be able to put a placeholder star with a candle on the set table to each diner.

If you liked this book and it was useful, I kindly ask you to leave me a review. I will be very grateful!

If you do not like it, if you have not understood something of the explanation or any other request, you can send me an email to this address and I'll answer right away: ilmiouncinettorosa@gmail.com
or you can contact me privately on my social networks.

I remind you of the contacts where you can follow me:

- **Instagram**: uncinetto_rosa
-
- **Fb**:https://www.facebook.com/uncinettorosasusy/
-
- **Etsy**:https://www.etsy.com/it/shop/UncinettoRosa?ref=shop_sugg

Printed in Great Britain
by Amazon